What Happens at a
Bakery?

by Kathleen Pohl

Reading consultant: Susan Nations, M.Ed., author/literacy coach/consultant in literacy development

Please visit our web site at: www.garethstevens.com
For a free color catalog describing Weekly Reader® Early Learning Library's list
of high-quality books, call 1-877-445-5824 (USA) or 1-800-387-3178 (Canada).
Weekly Reader® Early Learning Library's fax: (414) 336-0164.

Library of Congress Cataloging-in-Publication Data

Pohl, Kathleen.
     What happens at a bakery? / by Kathleen Pohl.
          p. cm. — (Where people work)
     Includes bibliographical references and index.
     ISBN-10: 0-8368-6884-6 — ISBN-13: 978-0-8368-6884-5 (lib. bdg.)
     ISBN-10: 0-8368-6891-9 — ISBN-13: 978-0-8368-6891-3 (softcover)
     1. Baking—Vocational guidance—Juvenile literature.   2. Bakers—Juvenile literature.
  I. Title.   II. Series: Pohl, Kathleen. Where people work.
     TX765.P64   2006
     664'.752—dc22   2006010589

This edition first published in 2007 by
Weekly Reader® Early Learning Library
A Member of the WRC Media Family of Companies
330 West Olive Street, Suite 100
Milwaukee, Wisconsin 53212 USA

Copyright © 2007 by Weekly Reader® Early Learning Library

Buddy® is a registered trademark of Weekly Reader Corporation.   Used under license.

Managing editor: Dorothy L. Gibbs
Art direction: Tammy West
Cover design and page layout: Scott M. Krall
Picture research: Diane Laska-Swanke and Kathleen Pohl
Photographer: Jack Long

Acknowledgments: The publisher thanks Jorge Lopez, Luis Gutierrez, and Raquel delaCruz Gutierrez
for modeling in this book. Special thanks to Jorge Lopez, of Lopez Bakery, for his expert consulting
and the use of his bakery's facilities.

Printed in the United States of America

1 2 3 4 5 6 7 8 9 10 09 08 07 06

Hi, Kids!

I'm Buddy, your Weekly Reader® pal. Have you ever visited a bakery? I'm here to show and tell what happens at a bakery. So, come on. Turn the page and read along!

A bakery smells so good! It is full of yummy things to eat. People love to shop at a bakery.

Mr. Lopez is a baker.
He bakes bread and
rolls. He bakes cakes
and cookies, too.

Today, Mr. Lopez is going to make twenty cakes! One of them will be a birthday cake for Luis.

First, Mr. Lopez makes **batter**. He uses lots of flour and sugar and eggs. He mixes them all in a big **mixer**.

mixer

Then he pours the batter into pans. He uses round pans and square pans and **sheet pans**.

sheet pan

The cakes bake in a big **oven**. They are very hot when they come out. The baker puts them on a tall **rack** to cool.

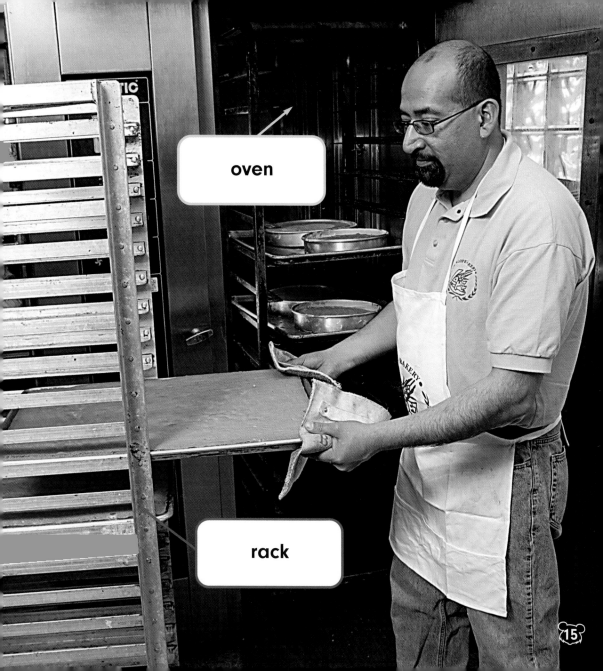

oven

rack

15

Now the cakes need frosting! Mr. Lopez **pipes** yellow frosting through the tip of a **frosting bag**. He makes a pretty border around Luis's cake.

frosting bag

Next, he fills the bag with red frosting. He uses other colors, too. He makes pictures on cakes with frosting.

Look at Luis's cake now!

Happy birthday, Luis.

🐻 Glossary

batter — a mixture of flour, sugar, eggs, water, and butter or oil that is thin enough to pour

border — a line or strip along the outside edge of something

frosting bag — a plastic bag with one corner cut off, where a special tip is attached for piping out frosting in different designs

pipes — pushes frosting out of a frosting bag to make a decorative pattern or design

sheet pans — large, flat baking pans for making big cakes that have only one layer

For More Information

Books

Bread Bakery. Read and Learn (series).
Catherine Anderson (Heinemann Library)

Jelly Beans from Start to Finish. Made in the USA (series).
Claire Kreger (Blackbirch Press)

Out and About at the Bakery. Jennifer A. Ericsson
(Picture Window Books)

Web Site

Bothams Kids Corner
www.botham.co.uk/kids.htm
The story behind a loaf of bread, plus games and recipes.

Publisher's note to educators and parents: Our editors have
carefully reviewed this Web site to ensure that it is suitable for children.
Many Web sites change frequently, however, and we cannot guarantee
that a site's future contents will continue to meet our high standards of
quality and educational value. Be advised that children should be closely
supervised whenever they access the Internet.

Index

About the Author

Kathleen Pohl has written and edited many children's books. Among them are animal tales, rhyming books, retold classics, and the forty-book series *Nature Close-Ups*. She also served for many years as top editor of *Taste of Home* and *Country Woman* magazines. She and her husband, Bruce, live among beautiful Wisconsin woods and share their home with six goats, a llama, and all kinds of wonderful woodland creatures.